IT'S OKAY

ISBN: 979-8-218-11124-3

Visit our website at: www.DynamicKidsPress.com

Published and printed in USA

Michael woke up in happy mood. He'd been waiting all week for soccer practice, and finally the day was here! Jumping up, he quickly put on his jersey and raced downstairs.

In the kitchen, Michael found Mom waiting with a stack of pancakes.

"Let's have some breakfast," she said. "Then, when you're done eating, we can take Harvey for a walk before school."

The three were headed toward the park a few minutes later when Harvey broke free and ran into a bush.

"Harvey! Come back!" Michael shouted. Crouching low, he climbed into the bush after Harvey.

Spying something shiny, Michael reached out for Harvey's collar. But his hands did not close on the collar. They closed on something else entirely!

It looked like a watch, but it was the strangest watch he'd ever seen.

Michael tried shaking the watch. He tried winding it and turning it around, but nothing happened.

From behind him, Michael heard Mom calling. "I found Harvey. Let's go home."

With a last look down, Michael stuffed the watch in his pocket. "Coming, Mom!"

Back at home, Michael tried again to make the watch work. He was so focused on it that he barely heard the phone ring.

A minute later, he felt a hand on his shoulder. "That was Coach," Mom said. "I'm sorry, Michael. He's not feeling well. Practice was cancelled today."

Sadness flooded Michael's body. He'd been looking forward
to soccer all morning. Now the whole day was ruined!
Letting out a loud groan, he ran to his room.
As he collapsed on the bed, he felt it.
The watch was BUZZING.

Michael looked down at the watch and nearly dropped it. There was someone there! "Who-who are you?" Michael asked.

"I am the Emotion Master. I'm here to help you understand your feelings.

Did you know that sadness is a blue emotion? So are disappointment and tiredness. It's okay to have blue emotions, but it's also important to help them pass. One of the best ways to do that is by talking about them."

Michael sighed. "What's the point. Talking about it won't change the fact that soccer was cancelled," Michael said.

The Emotion Master shrugged. "That's true. But it might help you to feel better about it. How will you know unless you try?"

Michael decided the Emotion Master was right. Going downstairs, he told his mom that he felt sad. "I really wanted to play today."

Mom gave him a big, warm hug. "Why don't you call Toby? You two can meet at the park and play soccer there?"

Michael grinned. That sounded great. And, he realized, talking *had* helped with his sadness.

"Toby! Pass the ball" Michael shouted. ZOOM! The ball flew high in the air, passed over Michael, and fell into the river.

"What did you do, Toby? Why did you kick the ball so high!" Michael said, anger filling his heart. His face turned red and his heart started to beat faster as he stormed away from his friend.

Suddenly, Michael's watch started to BUZZ again.

"Did you know that anger is a red emotion?" the Emotion Master said. "So are aggression, frustration, and feeling annoyed. It's okay to feel red emotions, sometimes, but then you have to let go of them. Try telling your friend why you are angry."

Michael nodded. Then, jogging back toward Toby, he said, "I'm sorry I yelled, Toby. I was angry because I was looking forward to playing soccer all morning, and now we've lost our ball!"

"I'm sorry, Michael," Toby said, his eyes growing wide. It was an accident! I was just trying to pass you the ball, but I kicked it way harder than I should have."
Michael's face softened. "It's okay. I know you didn't mean to do it."

"I have an idea!" Toby said. "How about if we play hide-and-seek instead. You hide, and I'll come and find you."

Michael's heart started to beat faster and skin tingled with excitement.

"Yeah!" he shouted. "Count to ten and I'll hide."

Turning Michael ran toward a tree. As he did so, he bumped into another kid.
"Watch it!" he shouted, and kept going.
Suddenly, Michael felt his watch buzzing again.

"Michael" the Emotion Master said, "I can see you're excited. That's a yellow emotion. So are being happy, playful, and surprised. But remember, you can be excited and polite at the same time."

At the Emotion Master's words, Michael realized he had been rude to the other kid.

"Hey, wait!" Michael called out. "I'm sorry I pushed you. I should have said excuse me, but I was too excited. Would you like to play hide-and-seek with us?"

The kid shook his head. "I've got to go home. But thanks, anyway!"

Michael and Toby played round after round of hide-and-seek. Finally, they heard Toby's mom calling to them.

"Time to go home," she said. "Michael's mom just called and asked me to drop him off."

At home, Michael hopped out of the car.
"Thanks for giving me a ride, Mrs. Brown. You were very kind."
Mrs. Brown smiled and waved goodbye to Michael.

"Michael!" Mom called as he came back inside.
"Why don't you go and change, and I'll get dinner ready."
Nodding, Michael rushed up the stairs just as his watch started to BUZZ again
"Did you know what you just did?"
Said the Emotion Master.
"What?" asked Michael.

"You thanked Toby's mom for being kind. That's called being thoughtful. It's a green emotion, just like being calm, patient, and peaceful."

Michael nodded his head. "Thank you for helping me understand my emotions today!"

That night, Michael lay in bed grinning from ear to ear.
His heart felt light and joyful. Michael's day hadn't gone as
he planned, but it had still turned out great.

The next morning when he woke up, Michael spotted the watch on his nightstand. Turning it over in his hands, he smiled to himself. He now understood his emotions, but not everyone did. It was time to pass on the watch.

Slipping on his coat and shoes, he called for Harvey.
"Come on, boy. Let's go for a walk. I've got something
to take to the park!"

Dear Grown-Up,

Next section contains fourteen short stories that describes a situation encountered by kids on a daily basis, followed by a negative and positive choice to choose from.

Read these short stories and discuss with your child how a positive and a negative choice will shape their day.

By reading these short stories you'll be able to empower kids to make positive choices while demonstrating the natural consequences to negative choices.

Enjoy!

Claire is playing a game with her little sister. They are happily sharing Claire's favorite toy, until her sister accidentally drops the toy and it breaks!

What would you do if you were Claire?

CHOICE 1   Get mad and break your sister's toy.

CHOICE 2   Stay calm and tell your sister it's okay.

David's mom tells him that he can't go and play at his friend's house today because his dad is going to come home early for a family dinner. David is upset because he was really looking forward to playing with his friend.

What would you do if you were David?

CHOICE 1   Tell your mom that you understand.

CHOICE 2   Tell your mom it's not fair and that she has to take you to your friend's house now.

Sally comes inside from playing and sees that she's tracked muddy footprints everywhere. She's worried that her parents will be very annoyed when they find out!

What would you do if you were Sally?

CHOICE 1 Blame it on someone else and say that you don't know how the footprints got there.

CHOICE 2 Clean the footprints and apologize.

Ben's friend at school has borrowed his favorite book and keeps forgetting to return it. Ben is annoyed because he really wants to read it again!

What would you do if you were Ben?

CHOICE 1 Get angry and tell your friend they have to bring it back.

CHOICE 2 Stay calm and ask your friend nicely to bring it back.

Tina just bought a brand-new toy from the toy store, but when she got home she couldn't find it anywhere! It must have gotten lost somewhere on the way home.

What would you do if you were Tina?

CHOICE 1   Tell your parents and ask for help finding it.

CHOICE 2   Get annoyed and demand a new toy.

Louis tried out for the lead in the school play, but it went to someone else. Instead, he got a smaller part.

Which would you do if you were Louis?

CHOICE 1   Feel annoyed that someone else was picked instead of you.

CHOICE 2   Feel excited about being in the school play.

Milly's dog has run away. Milly misses her dog a lot and doesn't know where she's gone.

How would you react in Milly's place?

CHOICE 1   Wallow in your room and cry about your missing dog.

CHOICE 2   Hang flyers and actively look for your dog.

Chris is in a shop with his mom when he realizes he can't see her anymore, no matter where he looks.

What would do if you were Chris?

CHOICE 1   Start to cry and run around trying to find her.

CHOICE 2   Find someone who works at the store and ask for help.

Martin is in bed. He's tired, but no matter what he does, he can't fall asleep.

What would you do if you were Martin?

CHOICE 1 Get annoyed that you can't sleep and shout for your parents to come.

CHOICE 2 Try to relax and make yourself feel comfortable.

Rose is at her piano lesson. She practiced all week to learn a song, but when she starts to play, she just can't seem to get it right.

What would you do if you were Rose?

CHOICE 1 Keep trying until you get it right.

CHOICE 2 Feel sad that you keep getting it wrong and give up trying.

Josh is painting a beautiful picture to give to his mom, but he gets so excited that the paint ends up going everywhere.

If you were Josh, what would you do?

CHOICE 1   Feel bad and try to hide what happened.

CHOICE 2   Tell your Mom right away and explain to her why it happened.

Jasmine is having fun playing at her friend's house. When her friend's dad makes her dinner, Jasmine sees that there's something on the plate that she doesn't like.

What would you do if you were Jasmine?

CHOICE 1   Refuse to eat anything on your plate and push it away.

CHOICE 2   Thank your friend's father for making dinner. Tell him that there's something you don't like, but eat everything else on the plate.

CHOICE 3   Taste food, then leave the rest if you don't like it.

Emily was invited to her friend's birthday party and she got a gift that she thinks her friend will really like. But when her friend opens the gift, she says that she already has it.

CHOICE 1 — Tell your friend that you didn't know she already had it and apologize.

CHOICE 2 — Feel upset and don't talk to your friend for the rest of the party.

Jessica and her brother are getting ready to go outside and play in the puddles. When she opens the door, she sees a huge toad and jumps back, which makes her brother laugh at her.

How would you react if you were Jessica?

CHOICE 1 — Tell your brother that it wasn't nice to laugh, then laugh at how silly the situation is yourself.

CHOICE 2 — Get embarrassed, stomp your feet, and refuse to play after all.

What emotions did the story teach you?
Michael is really excited to hear about it;
please provide feedback.

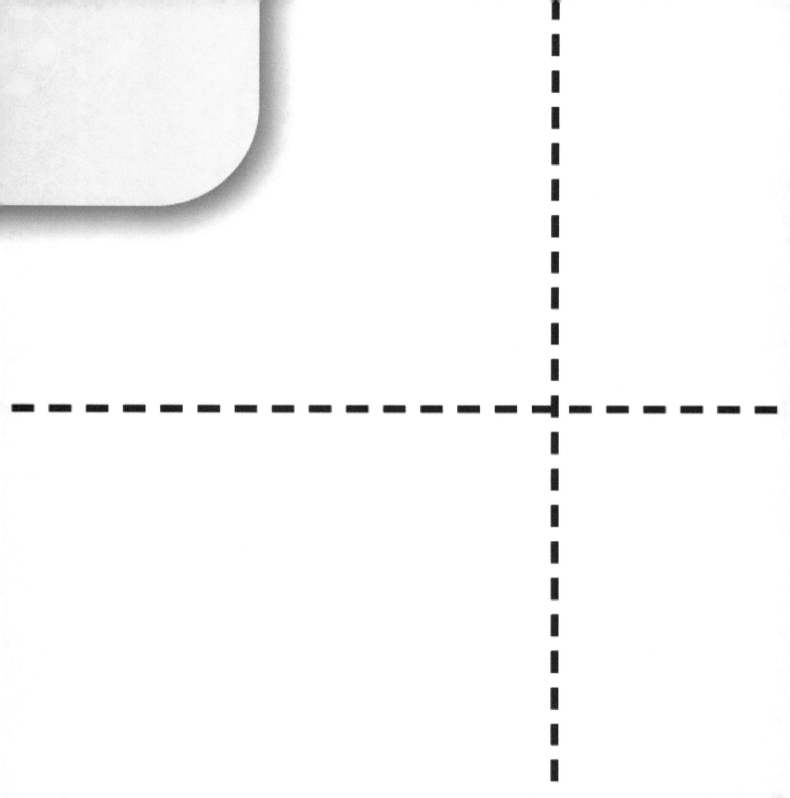

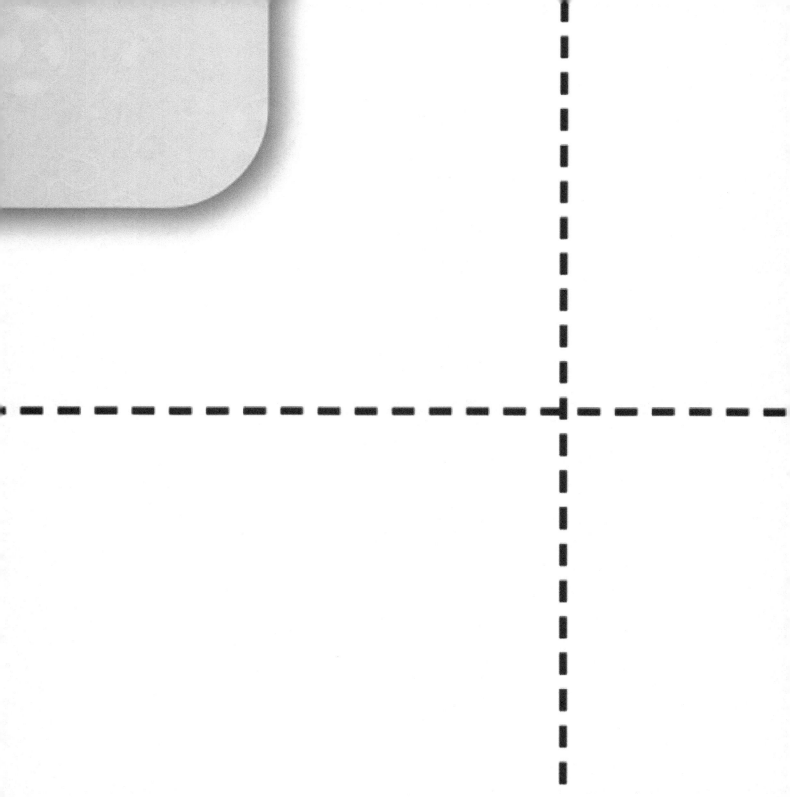

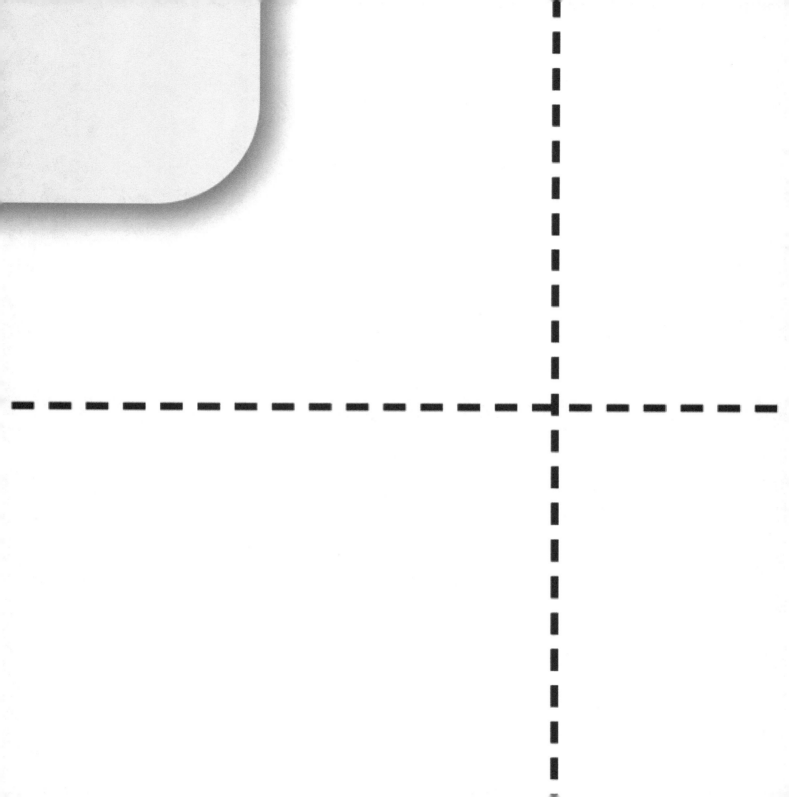

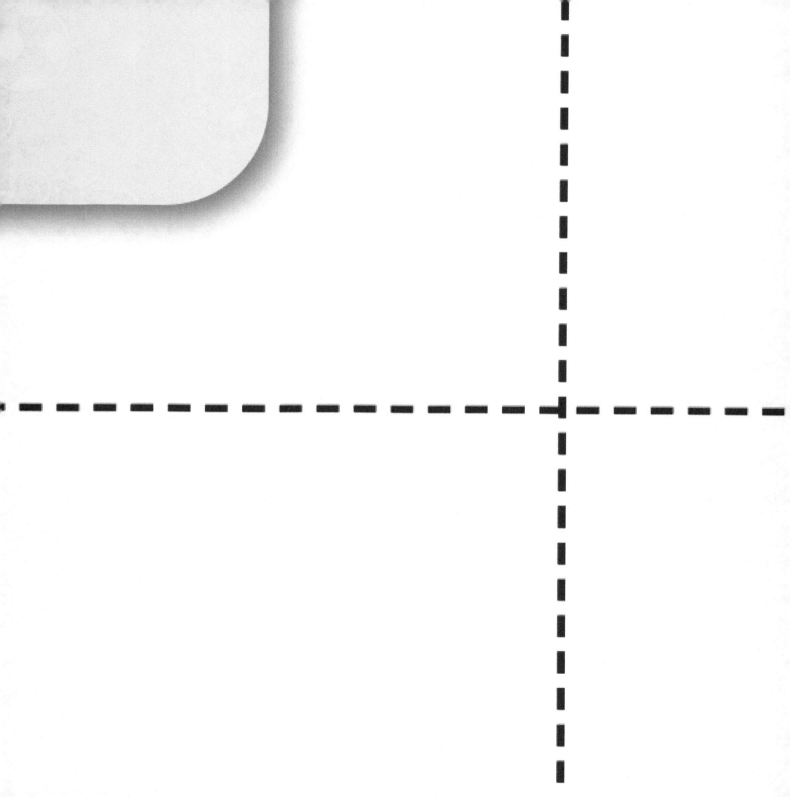

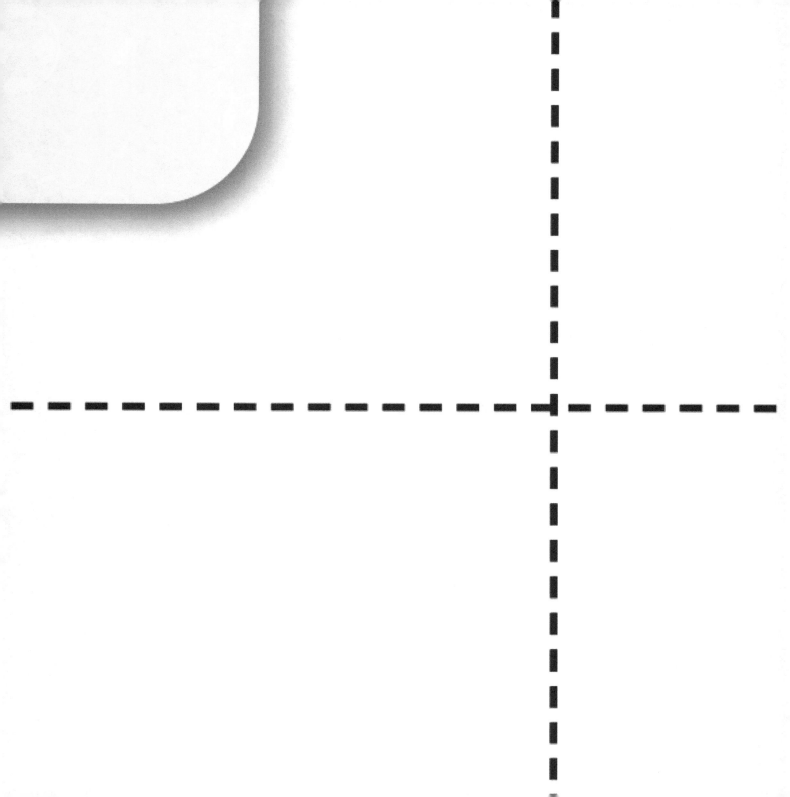

Surprised

Guilty

Happy

Angry

Proud

Sad

Scared

Tired

Excited

Worried

Disappointed

Hurt

Interested

Jealous

Thoughtful

Confused

Sick

Disgusted

Teasing

Silly

you,

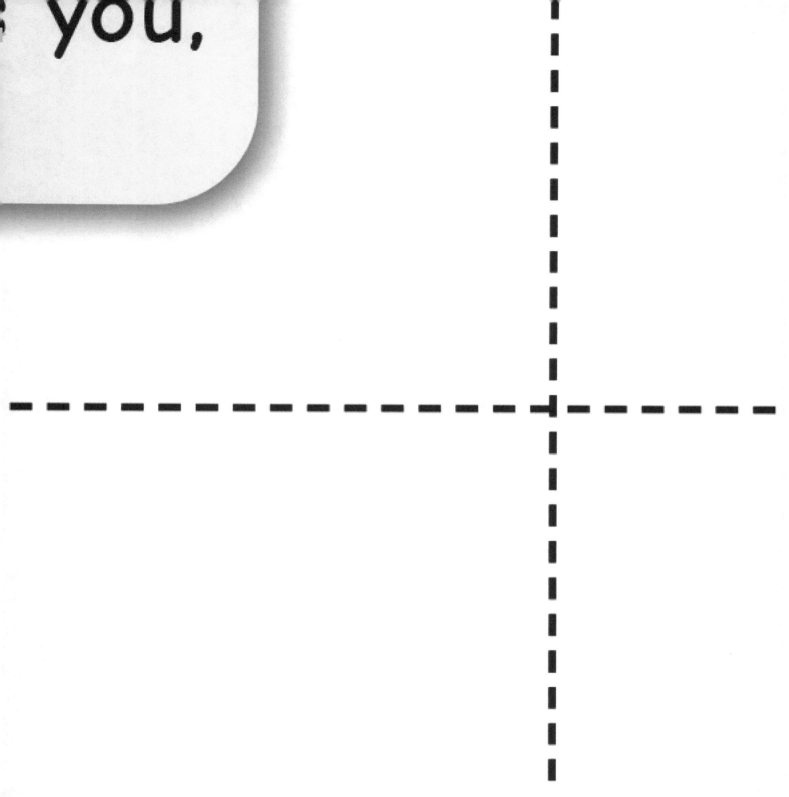

d.

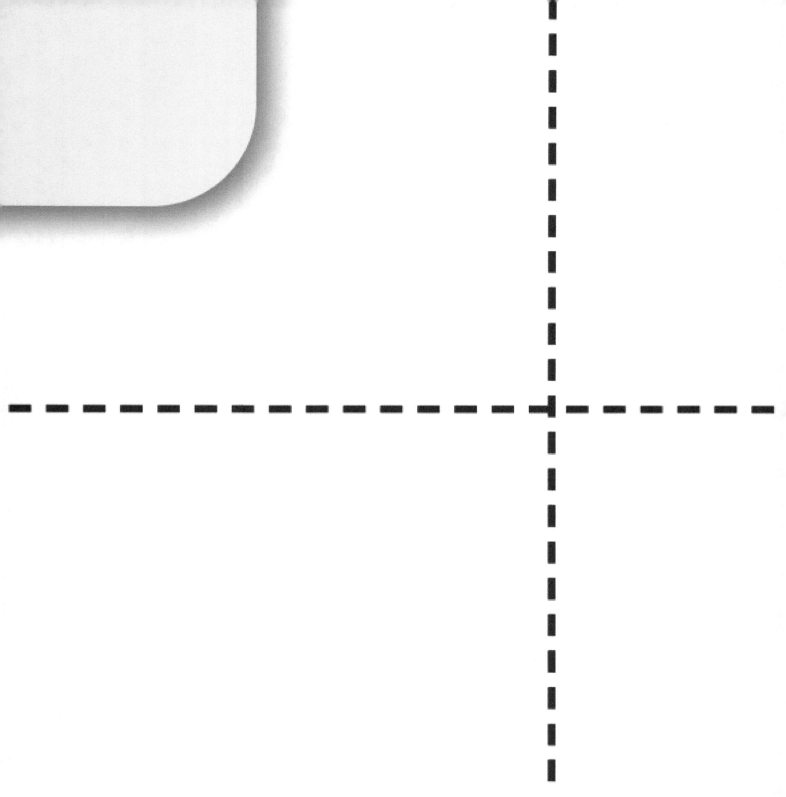

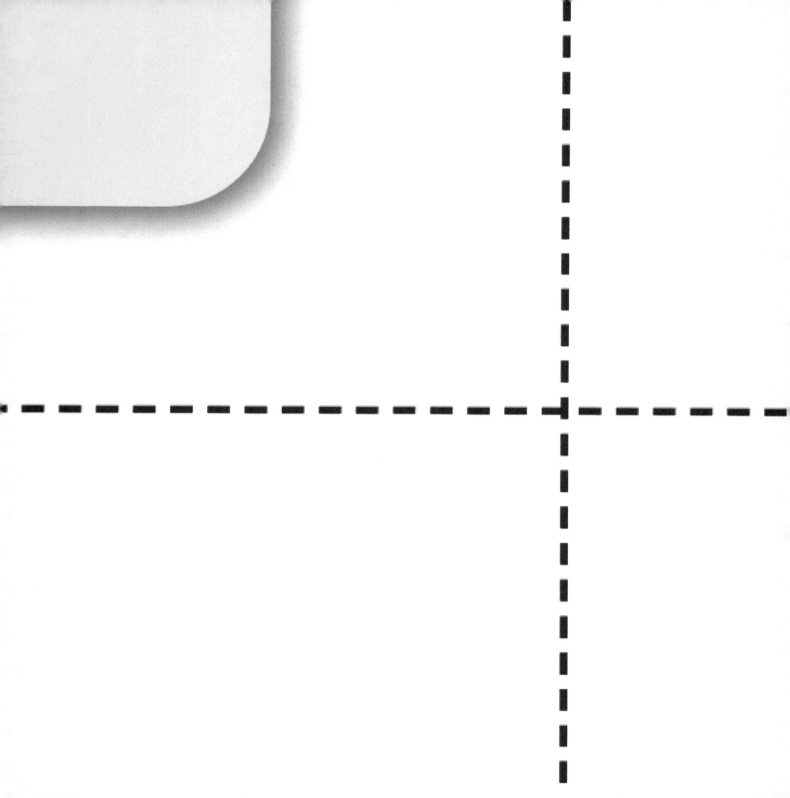

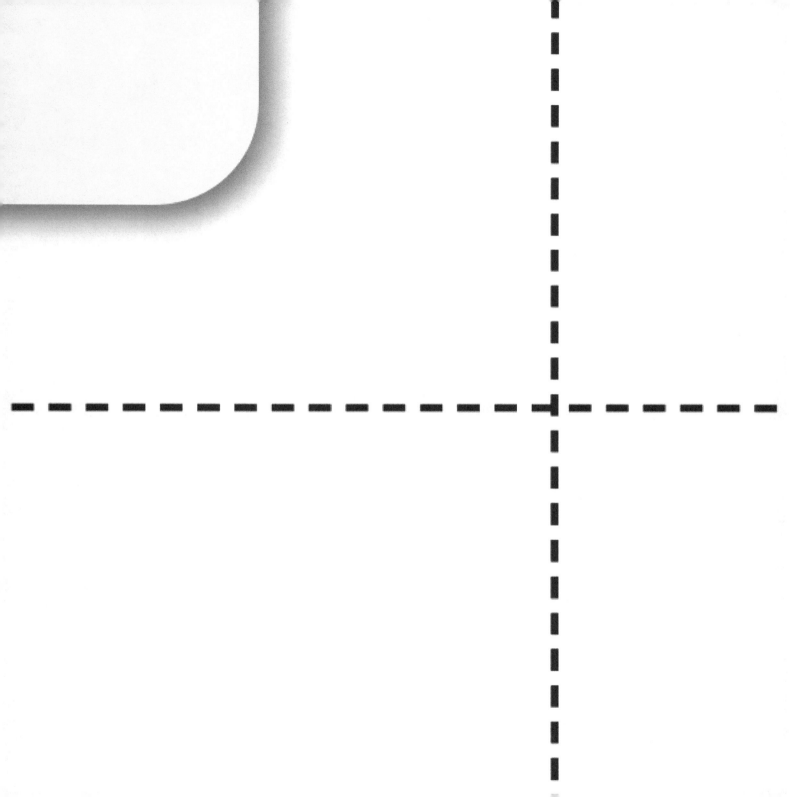

"Dear Grown-Up,

You can download these Emotion
Cards from our website at:

www.DynamicKidsPress.com/Ecards"

Made in the USA
Coppell, TX
13 August 2023

20296837R00044